Eric Kyper
Scott J. Lloyd

Improved Decision-making in Data Mining

Eric Kyper
Scott J. Lloyd

Improved Decision-making in Data Mining

A Heuristic Rule Induction Approach to Decision Tree Creation and Model Selection

VDM Verlag Dr. Müller

Impressum/Imprint (nur für Deutschland/ only for Germany)
Bibliografische Information der Deutschen Nationalbibliothek: Die Deutsche Nationalbibliothek
verzeichnet diese Publikation in der Deutschen Nationalbibliografie; detaillierte bibliografische
Daten sind im Internet über http://dnb.d-nb.de abrufbar.

Coverbild: www.purestockx.com

Verlag: VDM Verlag Dr. Müller Aktiengesellschaft & Co. KG
Dudweiler Landstr. 99, 66123 Saarbrücken, Deutschland
Telefon +49 681 9100-698, Telefax +49 681 9100-988, Email: info@vdm-verlag.de
Zugl.: Kingston, University of Rhode Island, Diss., 2006

Herstellung in Deutschland:
Schaltungsdienst Lange o.H.G., Berlin
Books on Demand GmbH, Norderstedt
Reha GmbH, Saarbrücken
Amazon Distribution GmbH, Leipzig
ISBN: 978-3-8364-8985-0

Imprint (only for USA, GB)
Bibliographic information published by the Deutsche Nationalbibliothek: The Deutsche
Nationalbibliothek lists this publication in the Deutsche Nationalbibliografie; detailed
bibliographic data are available in the Internet at http://dnb.d-nb.de.

Cover image: www.purestockx.com

Publisher:
VDM Verlag Dr. Müller Aktiengesellschaft & Co. KG
Dudweiler Landstr. 99, 66123 Saarbrücken, Germany
Phone +49 681 9100-698, Fax +49 681 9100-988, Email: info@vdm-publishing.com

Printed in the U.S.A.
Printed in the U.K. by (see last page)
ISBN: 978-3-8364-8985-0

Introduction

Model subset selection can be a difficult exercise even for experienced data analysts. This study presents an information criterion to aid in model subset selection for use with decision trees created from discretized datasets. Discretization is the process of transforming continuous data into ordinal categories (Benyon, 2004). Commonly used methods for discretization are *equal width intervals* and *equal frequency intervals*. Decision-makers often choose the number of categories to create based on convenience but without empirical, experimental or theoretical justification. The method of convenience often results in outputs not optimized for predictive accuracy or ease of interpretation. In data mining, decision trees are predictive models, that is, maps from observations about an item to conclusions about its target values. For discrete outcomes, they are often called *classification trees*. The leaves of these trees represent classification and the branches represent conjunctions of features that lead to classification. Because of its wide use in operational research management science (Kros, 2008), we present an information criterion to choose among the decision tree model subsets created by testing multiple categorization schemes. This could be for competing models generated from alternative discretization schemes (attribute-driven vs. entropy-driven), or from alternative outcomes generated by one scheme (differing frequencies in an equal frequency scheme). The decision tree information criterion facilitates tree (course of action in a decision matrix) selection by directly comparing the accuracy and complexities of decision trees in a given model subset. Efficient and accurate creation and comparison of multiple categorization schemes benefit decision-makers by precise results and knowledge of the opportunity losses among competitive model subsets.

1

We choose equal width interval algorithms because they create results that facilitate decision making, and are frequently used by data analysts. [For a complete discussion of the number of categories see Mitchell (1997) and Winston (1992).] While a variety of discretization algorithms have been presented in the literature, most of these are not readily available or easy to implement in common analysis software (ex. SAS, Statistica, Minitab).

Successful managers normally have an intuitive understanding of the decision-making process (Simon, 1987). Managers understand the tradeoff between accuracy and complexity (Simon, 1977) and the principle of *parsimony*. This principle represents managers' preferences, and we refer to it as Occam's Razor (Bozdogan, 1987; Moody, 1967). The parsimony principle states that simpler models are preferable to complex models, *ceteris paribus*. If a decision-maker knows the accuracy requirement for a given problem domain, then decision-makers benefit by having the simplest model (most parsimonious) to fulfill that requirement. However, decision-makers often do not have the time or ability to test multiple categorization schemes for a given dataset. In addition, decision-makers have a difficult time comparing the resulting models. The techniques below allow both the creation and comparison of multiple categorization schemes. As an example, requirements for accuracy known in advance are those that arise from legislation such as the Clean Air Act (1970) specifying air toxicity limits for industries.

As stated above, the need for model subset selection in decision trees is driven by two situations: trees generated from competing discretization schemes, and trees generated from multiple versions of a dataset within one discretization scheme. The proposed information criterion will suffice in both situations, but the pseudo-code presented in appendix A only addresses the former situation. We propose an information criterion that chooses among alternative decision trees. Furthermore, we propose a system to integrate the discretization and decision tree construction processes together into a single decision-making process. Essential to this process is the ability for decision-makers to understand alternative decision trees and quantify the opportunity losses associated with their decisions. Opportunity loss is the difference between the realized benefit of a course of action and the benefit of the optimal course of action. Opportunity loss is defined as, $O = A_i - A_o$. Where O is opportunity cost, A_i is the cost of an alternative, and A_0 is the cost of the optimal alternative. To meet this latter requirement, we develop a metric to evaluate and quantify the opportunity losses between sub-models (decision trees) of a dataset.

The proposed system may apply in many commercial situations. For example, an insurance company call center generates various statistics from the incoming calls including service levels and call volume. A decision tree provides information to quantify and rank the factors that influence service levels; this enables mangers to focus their efforts. Decision tree learning is generally best suited to problems with the following characteristics:

- Instances are represented by **attribute-value pairs**.
  - Instances described by a fixed set of attributes (e.g., temperature) and their values (e.g., hot).
  - The easiest situation for decision tree learning occurs when each attribute takes on a small number of disjoint possible values (e.g., hot, mild, cold).
  - Extensions to the basic algorithm allow handling real-valued attributes as well (e.g., a floating point temperature).
- The target function has **discrete output values**.

- A decision tree assigns a classification to each example.
  - Simplest case exists when there are only two possible classes (**Boolean classification**).
  - Decision tree methods can also be easily extended to learning functions with more than two possible output values.
- A more substantial extension allows learning target functions with real-valued outputs, although the application of decision trees in this setting is less common.
- Disjunctive descriptions may be required.
  - Decision trees naturally represent disjunctive expressions.
- The training data may contain errors.
  - Decision tree learning methods are robust to errors - both errors in classifications of the training examples and errors in the attribute values that describe these examples.
- The training data may contain missing attribute values.
  - Decision tree methods can be used even when some training examples have unknown values (e.g., humidity is known for only a fraction of the examples).

There is a large body of research detailing discretization/categorization methods. Discretizing continuous data involves two factors: (1) the number of intervals and (2) interval width. The techniques discussed below are methods to determine intervals and width respectively. For a complete understanding of the discretization literature see (Berka & Bruha, 1995; Besson, Robardet, Boulicaut, & Rome, 2005; Bryson & Joseph, 2001;

Dougherty, Kohavi, & Sahami, 1995; Ishibuchi & Yamamoto, 2003; Kurgan & Cios, 2004; Kwedlo & Kretowski, 1999; Liu, Wong, & Wang, 2004; Postema, Wu, & Menzies, 1997; Ventura & Martinez, 1995).

We organize the remainder of this book as follows; a discussion of the current decision-making literature and methodologies, model subset selection, information criterion for decision trees, opportunity loss, a real world example, and discussion/conclusion.

Decision-Making Literature/ Discretization Methodology

Choosing an appropriate discretization or categorization scheme is a non-trivial task that requires time and experience on behalf of the decision-maker. Moreover, statistical software, e.g., SAS, SPSS, Minitab and Statistica among others, have limited functionality for categorizing data beyond creating equal width intervals or equal frequency intervals. Using equal width intervals, we write a simple routine to repeatedly categorize a dataset into an increasing number of categories. Appendix A contains a sample of how to create multiple categories of equal width in Statistica[1] (this routine would be with minimal changes applied to SAS, SPSS, and Minitab). Once the dataset is categorized, our information criterion offers a simple way to then choose a resulting model that best fits the decision-makers specific needs.

According to Simon (1977, pp. pp. 57-58) the general process for using any mathematical tool in management decision-making contains the following steps:

1. "Construct a mathematical model that satisfies the conditions of the tool to be used and which, at the same time, mirrors the important factors in the management situation to be analyzed. For success, the basic structure

---

[1] Statistica 7.1, copyright© Statsoft, Inc. 1984-2005, see http://www.statsoft.com

of the tool must fit the basic structure of the problem, although compromise and approximation are often necessary to fit them to each other.

2. Define a criterion function, a measure to use for comparing the relative merits of various possible courses of action.

3. Obtain empirical estimates of the numerical parameters in the model that specify the particular, concrete situation to which it is to apply.

4. Carry through the mathematical calculations required to find the course of action, which, for the specified parameter values, maximizes the criterion function. With each of the tools are associated computational procedures for carrying out these calculations efficiently."

The above process outlines the steps used in this research. Once the collected data is in a format appropriate for analysis (categorized continuous variables), construction of decision trees begins. Step One above defines the important factors for study as accuracy and complexity. Step Two defines a criterion function; the information criterion presented below meets this requirement. Step Three requires the collection of empirical estimates for the criterion function parameters. We complete Step Three by collecting user preferences for evaluating between models as applied to their particular problem domain. Step Four applies calculations required to determine the desired course of action.

Model Subset Selection

If multiple categorization schemes are implemented the decision-maker has the real problem of choosing the appropriate model from the subset of models created. An often-cited solution in forecast evaluation is Akaike's Information Criterion (AIC). Akaike (1976) developed a criterion that chooses the simplest model for a given level of accuracy, thereby leading to parsimony. It is useful to briefly review Akaike's solution as a basis for comparison with the decision tree information criterion presented in the next section.

AIC selects from nested econometric or predictive models. The criterion is AIC = ln (s_m^2) + 2m/T, where m is the number of parameters in the model; s_m^2 is the estimated residual variance (in an autoregressive example), and T is the number of observations. The criterion minimizes over choices of m forming a tradeoff between model fit and model complexity (measured by m) (Wei, 1993). The basic components of this model are accuracy and complexity, measured by s_m^2 and m respectively. Finally, AIC selects the simplest model subset having the greatest accuracy.

To calculate a measure of parsimony for decision trees the proposed information criterion (referred to from now on as IC) evaluates decision tree accuracy and complexity respectively. One possible method to measure decision tree complexity is through an implementation of Shannon's information theory research (Shannon, 1948). Information theory specifies the measurement of complexity of information when choices are not equally likely. Shannon developed the method to measure the average number of bits required to describe an entity. In the simplest form M: bits = $\log_2 M$, where M is the number of choices. In decision trees, a binary decision is made at each non-terminal node. This study uses the criterion developed by Shannon to measure complexity in decision trees. The number of non-terminal nodes now represents the number of possible choices. Therefore, decision tree complexity becomes $\log_2 N$, where N = number of non-terminal nodes.

Statistica provides the mean square error (MSE) as a measure of accuracy with predictive decision trees. Traditional prediction methods, for example ordinary least squares regression, employ R^2, the coefficient of determination (proportion of total variation explained by the model), as a measure of accuracy. While not generally associated with decision trees, there exists no statistical obstacle to calculating R^2.

$$R^2 = \frac{\sum_{i=1}^{n}(\hat{Y} - \bar{Y})^2}{\sum_{i=1}^{n}(Y - \bar{Y})^2}, \text{ where } \hat{Y} \text{ is the predicted value, } Y \text{ is the observed value, and } \bar{Y} \text{ is the}$$

mean of the observed values. We provide the required predicted and observed values for these decision trees. Additionally, R^2 is bound to $(0 \leq R^2 \leq 1)$, making the interpretation of the IC straightforward. Thus, it is a measure of relative accuracy where 1 is perfect accuracy. With working measures for accuracy and complexity, one constructs a ratio. We detail the calculation of this ratio in the next section.

Decision Tree Information Criterion

Once we define measures of accuracy and complexities, it is possible to construct a ratio of accuracy to complexity (similar to AIC). It is easier to define the functions for accuracy and complexity independently than to construct the IC measure right away.

The accuracy function chosen in this study is $1-R^2$, "the numerator", (decreases with R^2). This function is a complement of R^2, making low IC values desirable. This means that the numerator will have low values at high levels of accuracy. In this case, perfect accuracy ($R^2 = 1$) would have a numerator of zero and a total lack of accuracy would have a numerator of 1.

8

The complexity function chosen in this study is $N/(1-\log_2 N)$. This function decreases with N. This has implications for constant levels of accuracy. As N increases, the complexity function decreases and correspondingly the IC function will increase. This is a penalty since low values of IC are desirable.

The IC measure is COMPLEXITY*ACCURACY, $N\ (1-R^2)/\ (1-\text{Log}_2 N)$. This expression yields negative values, so its complement is taken, yielding positive values to facilitate interpretation: $1 - N\ (1-R^2)/\ (1-\log_2 N)$. Taking the common denominator $1-\log_2 N$ yields

$$IC = \frac{[1 - \log_2 N - N(1 - R^2)]}{[1 - \log_2 N]} \qquad (1)$$

To encapsulate the decision-maker's input, we add two additional parameters to the equation resulting in

$$IC = \frac{[1 - \log_2 \kappa(N)] - [(N)(1 - \psi R^2)]}{1 - \log_2 \kappa(N)} \qquad (2)$$

For values greater than zero, ψ parameter adjusts the benefit of accuracy and the κ parameter adjusts the penalty of complexity. To examine the function in each dimension, we find the derivatives of the function. Graphical representations of the function follow the discussion on derivatives.

Derivatives:

Let $u = 1-\log_2 \kappa N$. Equation is then $DTIC = \dfrac{[u - N(1 - \psi R^2)]}{u}$

The partial derivative with respect to R^2 (< 0 for all $\kappa N \geq 2$) is

$$\frac{\delta IC}{\delta R^2} = \frac{N}{u} = \frac{N\psi}{(1 - \log_2 \kappa N)} \qquad (3)$$

Note that the rate of change of IC with respect to R^2 (the above derivative) is negative and a function of N. More precisely, u is negative for $\log_2 \kappa N > 2$, so N/u is negative for the same value. Lower values of IC indicate better accuracy, and the response of the function to R^2 increases with N. The implications are that for constant levels of accuracy (R^2), as complexity increases (N), the values of IC increase (becoming less desirable).

Second partial derivative with respect to R^2 (slope with respect to R^2 is constant):

$$\frac{\delta^2 IC}{\delta^2 R^2} = 0 \qquad (4)$$

This confirms that the slope of the previous derivative does not change. This indicates that the response of the function to R^2 does not change as N changes.

First partial derivative with respect to N:

$$\frac{\delta IC}{\delta N} = \frac{[u - N(1 - \psi R^2)]du - u[du - (1 - \psi R^2)]}{u^2} = \qquad (5.0)$$

$$\frac{u du - N(1 - \psi R^2)du - u du + (1 - \psi R^2)u}{u^2} = \qquad (5.1)$$

$$\frac{(1 - \psi R^2)(u - Ndu)}{u^2} \qquad (5.2)$$

This has an extremum at u – Ndu = 0, or **u = Ndu**

Second partial derivative with respect to N:

$$\frac{\delta^2 IC}{\delta N^2} = \frac{(1 - \psi R^2)[(u - Ndu)(2udu) - u^2(du - (Nd^2u + du))]}{u^4} = \qquad (6.0)$$

$$\frac{(1 - \psi R^2)(2u^2 du - 2Nudu^2 - u^2 du + u^2 Nd^2 u + u^2 du)}{u^4} = \qquad (6.1)$$

$$\frac{(1 - \psi R^2)(2u^2 du - 2Nudu^2 + u^2 Nd^2 u)}{u^4} \qquad (6.2)$$

The above expression evaluated at u =Ndu, with du= $\dfrac{-\log_2 e}{N}$ and $d^2 u = \dfrac{\log_2 e}{N^2}$

yields:

$$\frac{(1-\psi R^2)(\log_2 e)^2}{N}(-\log_2 e + 2N) \tag{7}$$

which is > 0 for N ≥ 1, MINIMUM at u =Ndu.

Note that the rate of change with respect to N is a function of both N and R^2; it has a minimum at U=Ndu, (which is at $N = (1/\kappa)2^{Log2e\,+\,1} = 5.437/\kappa$) and increases thereafter. The slope is negative before, zero at the point u=Ndu, and positive thereafter resulting in a minimum shaped like a valley (see Figure 2). The IC function has a local minimum of $5.4/\kappa$ when N = 5. This creates difficulties in distinguishing between trees where N<5. However, previous research suggests that trees that small are rare in reality (see Cherkauer & Shavlik, 1996). In addition, there is a global minimum at IC = 1 when we achieve $[R^2 = 1/\psi]$.

To visualize the behavior of the function, the breadth (dimension) is modeled separately in three directions. Figure 1 below shows the shape of the gain function (fixed complexity). Input tables for Figures 1 thru 3 are in Appendix B. The gain function is decreasing linearly, with a minimum of IC = 1 at $R^2 = 1$. This demonstrates that greater values of R^2 result in lower IC values, and that perfect accuracy results in a global minimum IC of 1.0.

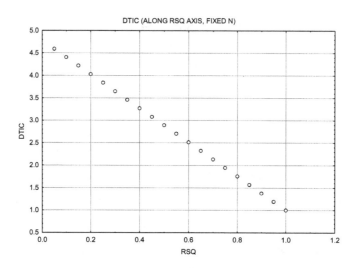

Figure 1: Accuracy function holding complexity constant

Figure 2 below shows the shape of the penalty function, which demonstrates that for nodes greater than 5, increasing complexity results in greater values of IC.

12

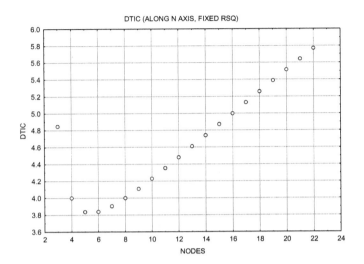

Figure 2: Complexity function holding accuracy constant

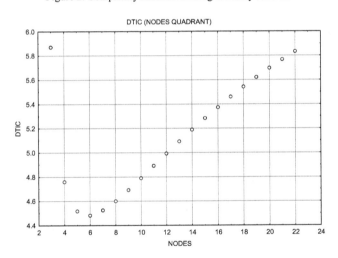

Figure 3: Simultaneously varying complexity and accuracy

13

Figure 3 demonstrates the J-shaped curve frequently produced by the measurement function (Appendix B provides empirical evidence to support this). In all cases, the IC function produces a global minimum. In the above case, a model with six nodes (barring any decision-maker input) has the optimal tradeoff between accuracy and complexity as defined by the IC. This demonstrates the measurement's natural tendency towards more parsimonious models for a constant increase in accuracy and complexity. In practice, the increases in accuracy and complexity are not always linear. This creates no problems in calculating the IC or modeling decision trees, but means that the IC function does not behave monotonically with changes in R^2 and the number of non-terminal nodes.

Opportunity Loss

Cyert, Simon, and Trow (1956, p. pp. 237) outline the importance of choosing between alternatives in decision-making. They describe an economic rational choice process as:

1. "An individual is confronted with a number of different, specified alternative courses of action.

2. To each of these alternatives is attached a set of consequences that will ensue if that alternative is chosen.

3. The individual has a system of preferences or "utilities" that permit him to rank all sets of consequences according to preference and to choose that alternative that has the preferred consequences. In the case of business decisions, the criterion for ranking is generally assumed profit."

However, according to Cyert, Simon, and Trow (1956, p. pp. 237) several missing elements must be incorporated into the above process. These missing elements are:

1. "The alternatives are not usually "given" but must be sought, and hence it is necessary to include the search for alternatives as an integral part of the process.

2. The information as to what consequences are attached to which alternatives is seldom "given," but, instead, the search for consequences is another important segment of the decision-making task.

3. We do not make comparisons among alternatives in terms of simple, single criterion like profit maximization. One reason is that there are often important consequences that are so intangible as to make an evaluation in terms of profit difficult or impossible. In place of searching for the "best" alternative, the decision-maker is usually concerned with finding a satisfactory alternative - one that will attain a specified goal and at the same time satisfy a number of auxiliary conditions.

4. Often, in the real world, the problem itself is not a "given", but, instead, searching for significant problems to which organizational attention should be turned becomes an important organizational task."

The IC presented above is effective at choosing between alternative decision trees and satisficing a decision-maker's preference for either accuracy or parsimony. Satisficing decides on a course of action that meets the minimum requirements to achieve a goal. To compare the consequences of choosing one decision tree over another requires a new yet undefined measure. To state the consequences in terms of profit, an intimate understanding of the problem domain is needed, but not likely known. The IC is robust enough to be applied across most, if not all, problem domains. The measure of consequences then must share the same quality.

Applying the concept of opportunity loss (Petersen & Lewis, 1999) creates a generalizable measure of the consequences between trees which is easy for decision-makers to understand. The difference in mean values of the response variables between trees (model subsets) is often very small, resulting in a poor measure of opportunity loss. Even with small differences in mean response values, the variance of the individual means within a tree differs a great deal between model subsets. Calculating the difference in root mean square errors (RMSE) for the model with the lowest IC and the competing models, accounts for the cost of choosing between alternative models. The RMSE is calculated as $\sqrt{\dfrac{\sum(\hat{y}-y)^2}{N}}$, where $\hat{y}$ are the predicted values, y are the observed values, and N is the number of observations (McClave, Benson, & Sincich, 2001). The RMSE is the residual after we define all modeled relationships. We apply this when looking for differences between sub-models. Positive values indicate the competing model has response values with greater variation. Negative values indicate the competing model has response values with less variation.

While the IC is capable of measuring the tradeoff between accuracy and complexity of decision trees (parsimony), comparing IC values has little meaning for decision-makers. This is because the IC values represent a complex relationship between accuracy and complexity, and are extremely difficult to comprehend in any sense other than knowing some trees had higher values than others did.

R^2 is calculated for each decision tree. This gives a precise measure for goodness of fit for each tree. However, it is difficult for a user to convert that measure of goodness of fit into actual differences in response values between trees. The differences in **root mean square deviation** (RMSE) between trees simplify arriving at a decision by indicating the accuracy of prediction of mean values at each non-terminal node.

Real World Example

A review of the relevant literature shows that the majority of researchers in the area of discretization agree it belongs in the pre-processing stage. It also demonstrates the lack of algorithms capable of handling sophisticated user input (some do allow the specification of the number of intervals), the lack of performance metrics, and clearly indicates that researchers are not viewing this problem from a decision-making point of view.

In our previous research (Kyper, Lloyd, & Chinn, 2004) we outlined the importance of discretization for use in data mining, specifically with rough sets and tree induction. Discretization is the process of transforming continuous data into ordinal categories. There are a variety of discretizers; the most commonly used are *equal width intervals* and *equal frequency intervals*. Choosing among various discretization methods is a time-consuming task and results in decision trees with varying levels of accuracy and complexity. This study presents a decision tree information criterion to evaluate predictive decision trees. Throughout this book the term decision tree refers specifically to binary decision trees. Tree evaluation is necessary under two situations. Choosing among decision trees discretized with different algorithms, and choosing among decision trees discretized with an algorithm that can create multiple categorization schemes (e.g. equal width intervals). Choosing among various models (decision trees) produced from the same dataset is called model subset selection. The decision tree information criterion will facilitate tree selection by directly comparing accuracy and complexities of decision trees in a given model subset.

The decision trees in this study rely upon continuous data discretized with an *equal width interval* algorithm. We chose equal width interval algorithm because it creates results that facilitate decision-making, is easy to use and understand, and is commonly available in decision tree software.

Successful managers have an intuitive understanding of the decision making process (Simon, 1987). These managers understand the tradeoff between accuracy and complexity (Simon, 1977). The principle of *parsimony* represents managers' preferences in this tradeoff, and is sometimes referred to as Occam's Razor (Bozdogan, 1987; Moody, 1967). The proposed decision tree information criterion automates the process of choosing between decision trees based on discretized data. The proposed system integrates the discretization and decision tree construction processes together into a single decision-making process. Essential to this process is the ability for decision-makers to understand alternative decision trees and quantify the opportunity losses associated with their decisions.

We define Opportunity Loss as the difference between the realized benefit of a course of action and the benefit of the optimal course of action (Jarrett & Kraft, 1989, p. pp. 639). Opportunity loss is defined as, $O = A_i - A_o$. Where O is opportunity cost, A_i is the cost of an alternative, and A_0 is the cost of the optimal alternative. To meet this latter requirement a metric to evaluate and quantify the opportunity losses between sub-models (decision trees) of a dataset is developed and presented below.

Any process that collects continuous data is a potential candidate for this application. For example, an insurance company call center generates various statistics from the incoming calls. These include date, time, service levels, call volume, and handle times. A decision tree provides information to quantify and rank the factors that influence service levels; this enables mangers to focus their efforts. Decision trees also permit managers to forecast future service levels based on current performance. Attributes such as call volume are not categorical in nature, they must first be discretized. The system proposed below provides a means to discretize, analyze, and choose between competing models based on an individual manager's needs.

Our purpose is in turn, to automate the discretization, the analysis of decision tree, information criterion (IC) evaluation, and opportunity loss calculations. One goal is to establish the validity and reliability of the IC and opportunity loss measure. Towards that end, we evaluate our process with service level data obtained from an insurance call center for a American insurance company. Since managers concern themselves with optimizing courses of action in the face of uncertainty, the analysis and results sections focus on how the program facilitates improved managerial decision-making.

Program Outline

Statistica[2] Visual Basic (an implementation of visual basic for applications within Statistica) was used to create an application to discretize data, pass the discretized data to

---

[2] Statistica 7.1, copyright© Statsoft, Inc. 1984-2005, see http://www.statsoft.com

CART (classification and regression trees), evaluate the results with the IC, and calculate opportunity losses, which is the loss associated with choosing a non-optimal decision. The application contains three sections: (1) discretization, (20 decision tree creation and (3) decision tree evaluation.

Discretization: We develop data subsets using equal width intervals for decision variables (Anderson, Sweeney, and Williams, 2005, pp 33-34). Preliminary analysis demonstrates that the IC does not choose models with more than 50 discretized categories for this dataset. For this reason, the IC application defaults to creating 50 categories, however, the user may increase this number. The number of equal width intervals created starts at 5 and increments by 5 until a maximum of 50 intervals is achieved.

Decision Tree Creation: Once all continuous variables are in discrete form, we pass the data to the CART procedure. The CART results provided contains all the necessary components to calculate the IC and opportunity loss measure. The output includes the number of terminal/non-terminal nodes, and the actual and predicted values for each observation. The decision tree information criterion formula is:

$$\textit{Decision Tree Information Criterion: } IC = \frac{[1 - \log_2 N - N(1 - \psi R^2)]}{[1 - \log_2 N]}$$, where N is the

number of non-terminal nodes. The IC accomplishes the task of selecting the model subset with the best tradeoff between accuracy and complexity. User input influences this selection through the manipulation of ψ, the accuracy parameter.

The sequence diagram in Figure 1 below shows the order of program calls in the application, and Appendix C contains pseudo-code for this application.

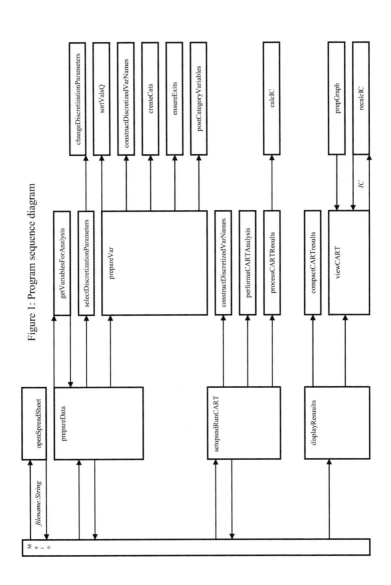

Figure 1: Program sequence diagram

Data Overview

Collected data was provided by a national insurance company's call center operations. As part of the agreement to gather the data, the identity of the firm is withheld. Managers for the call center concern themselves with factors affecting service levels. The following data are collected:

- DATE: date of service

- TIME: hour of day ranging from 9:00 AM to 7:00 PM (one hour increments)

- SERVICELV: service level, the percent of calls answered within a given number of seconds (see Atlason, Epelman, & Henderson, 2004)

- CALLS: equals the number of calls answered

- ABANDONED: callers who hung up before being answered

- AHT: average handle time in seconds including the call time and wrap up time after the call concludes

- ASA: average speed of answer in seconds

- MAX DELAY: maximum delay, the time in seconds the longest call waited until either answered or hung up

	Mean	Median	Std.Dev.
SERVICELV	0.922	0.933	0.079
CALLS	2017.577	2004.000	1275.036
ACD CALLS	2008.485	1995.000	1269.089
ABANDONS	9.092	6.000	14.567
AHT	298.447	301.000	25.229
ASA	7.488	6.000	11.471
MAXDELAY	178.977	133.000	168.777

Table 1: Descriptive statistics for selected variables

Variables date and time are not included in Table 1 because descriptive statistics do not apply, but they are transformed for use (see below). As can be seen the call center has an average SERVICELV of 92%, with a standard deviation of 8%. Since the mean and median are close the variables approximate normality, accordingly 95% of SL's lie between 76% - 100% (+/- 2 standard deviations).

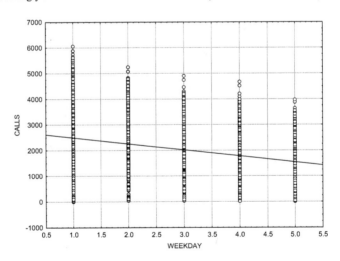

Figure 2: Call volume vs. weekday

Figure 2 above shows the distribution of calls by weekday. Volume steadily decreases from Monday to Friday. The variable date is transformed to weekday with values 1 - 5 corresponding to Monday through Friday respectively.

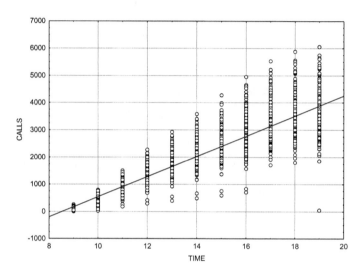

Figure 3: Call volume vs. time of day

Figure 3 displays the distribution of calls by time of day and shows that call volume steadily increases during the day. Time of day is presented hourly using a 24 hour clock.

	Bolded correlations are sig. at p < .05								
	DATE	WKDAY	TIME	SL	CALLS	ABNDNS	AHT	ASA	MAXDLY
DATE	1.00	-0.02	-0.01	0.01	**-0.06**	**-0.04**	**-0.15**	**-0.05**	**0.11**
WEEKDAY	-0.02	1.00	-0.01	**0.16**	**-0.26**	**-0.17**	**0.08**	**-0.13**	-0.02
TIME	-0.01	-0.01	1.00	0.00	**0.92**	**0.35**	**0.31**	0.02	**0.39**
SERVICELV	0.01	**0.16**	0.00	1.00	**-0.04**	**-0.67**	**-0.07**	**-0.87**	**-0.42**
CALLS	**-0.06**	**-0.26**	**0.92**	**-0.04**	1.00	**0.41**	**0.30**	0.04	**0.35**
ABANDONS	**-0.04**	**-0.17**	**0.35**	**-0.67**	**0.41**	1.00	**0.14**	**0.76**	**0.51**
AHT	**-0.15**	**0.08**	**0.31**	**-0.07**	**0.30**	**0.14**	1.00	**0.06**	**0.14**
ASA	**-0.05**	**-0.13**	0.02	**-0.87**	0.04	**0.76**	**0.06**	1.00	**0.43**
MAXDELAY	**0.11**	-0.02	**0.39**	**-0.42**	**0.35**	**0.51**	**0.14**	**0.43**	1.00

Table 2: Correlations matrix

A correlation analysis on all variables yields the results in Table 2. The results shows date and time do not correlate with service level although call volume correlates with both variables (at significance levels of .05 or less). Intuitively it makes sense that service level quality would suffer during high call volume times and excel during low call volume times. However, a quick analysis shows that is not the case.

To simplify the analysis, we remove predictor variables time and date, which do not correlate with service level from the analysis. The revised data set includes: service level (SERVICELV), weekday, calls, abandons, average handle time (AHT), average speed of answer (ASA), and max delay (MAXDELAY).

Analysis/ Results

For each analysis, SERVICELV is the response variable, WEEKDAY is a categorical variable, and the continuous predictor variables are CALLS, ABANDONS, AHT, ASA, and MAXDELAY; 2777 valid observations exist for this data set. Each continuous variable will be discretized 10 times into categories ranging from 5 to 50 in increments of 5. This results in 10 CART analyses, one for each set of categories. Initial results for the dataset are presented in Table 4 below.

Cats	NTN	R^2	IC	Opportunity Loss
5	19	0.646	3.071	0.009
10	18	0.705	2.673	0.004
30	16	0.712	2.535	0.004
15	**17**	**0.764**	**2.301***	**0.038**

Table 3: Results for dataset with parameter value 1.0

Table 3 does not contain categories 20, 25, 35, 40, 45, or 50 because those models have the same number of non-terminal nodes as the models that appear in the table. If two models have the same complexity (number of non-terminal nodes) only the model with the higher accuracy is kept. This is useful for decision-makers because it provides a reduced subset of models. In this dataset, we reduced the model subset 10 to 4.

Table 3 shows the number of categories created for each continuous variable, the number of non-terminal nodes, coefficient of determination ($R^{2)}$, the IC value, and a measure of opportunity loss expressed in terms of root mean square error (RMSE) differences. The model with the lowest IC value and an accuracy parameter of 1.0 is bolded and contains an asterisk beside the IC value. This represents the model with the most efficient tradeoff between accuracy and complexity as defined by the IC function. Observe an actual RMSE value as an example for the bolded model. The remaining values in the RMSE column are the differences between that value and the other RMSE's.

26

The model chosen contains 15 categories for each continuous variable, 17 non-terminal nodes, has an R^2 of .76, and an RMSE of .038. The opportunity loss column shows no trees exist with less variation of the predicted response variable at each terminal node. The competing models have at least a .004 increase in RMSE. An increase in RMSE is undesirable because it is accompanied by an increase in variance of the response variable. Figure 4 below shows a graph of the relationship between the number of non-terminal nodes and the IC values. This relationship graphs as a J curve, with the chosen model on the less complex end of the X axis (non-terminal nodes).

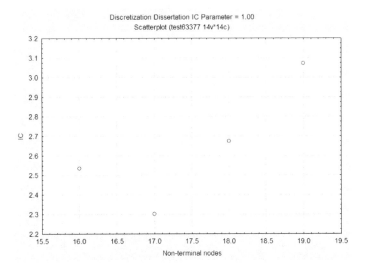

Figure 4: Non-terminal nodes vs. IC, for IC parameter 1.00

This application offers the user the option to change the parameter value (ψ) thus altering the accuracy parameter of the IC function. Possible input values range

27

from 0.1 to 2.0 in increments of .1. A value of 2.0 would weight accuracy twice as heavily as a value of 1.0. Conversely a value of 0.1 weights accuracy one tenth as heavily as a value of 1.0. The optimal parameter value for each call center is impossible to learn from the analyzed data because it depends upon an individual decision-maker's preference for parsimony. For illustrative purposes, we test the parameter value at each extremum. Initially, we utilize the default value 1.0. Testing indicated for this dataset that the choice of any parameter value greater than 1.0 does not affect the results; hence, the procedure does not duplicate the upper extremum results. A parameter value of 0.1 chooses the least complex decision tree and is appropriate for decision-makers who desire a parsimonious model and are less concerned with accuracy. Table 4 below shows for a parameter value of 0.1, the resulting tree has 30 categories for each continuous variable, 16 non-terminal nodes, an R^2 of .71, and RMSE of .042.

Cats	NTN	R^2	IC	Opportunity Loss
30	16	0.71	5.95*	0.042

Table 4: Resulting model with parameter value 0.10

If one alters a parameter value, the program recalculates all the IC values in the reduced model subset, and you observe the model with the resulting lowest IC. Figure 5 below shows the recalculated IC values and their corresponding tree sizes. The new relationship between IC and the number of non-terminal nodes is now linear as opposed to the previous curvilinear relationship.

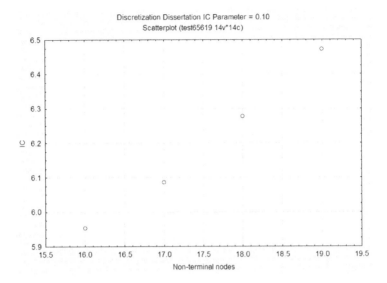

Figure 5: Non-terminal nodes vs. IC, for IC parameter 0.10

Decision-Making Implications

This program provides decision-makers a method to automatically discretize a dataset, construct decision trees, and then compare decision trees with the IC and opportunity loss measure. The decision-maker can be confident that the program removes all trees with equal complexity and lower accuracy. This provides a good starting point from which to choose a model that satisfies the decision-maker's preference for parsimony.

This proposed automated process aids management decision-making in two ways: First, decision-makers can study the tree and isolate the variables affecting the response variable service level. Examining Figure 6 shows that of the six variables entered into the analyses only five are included in the decision tree: mean

29

(average) handle time, mean (average) speed of answer, abandons, maximum delay, and weekday. This provides managers with information regarding the importance of collected data. Second, we do not include call volume in the decision tree because it does not correlate with service level. The analysis suggests managers should focus on improving the treatment of existing calls instead of focusing on reducing call volume.

Earlier we discussed the economic rational choice process (Cyert et al., 1956). The final step in that process involves searching for problems to which an organization should focus their attention. By using the presented decision tree, managers are able to see if service levels are a priority, then attention should focus on the factors that clearly affect service level. This suggests that further study of each factor is necessary to determine the extent of the organization's influence over the factor. Average speed of answer is a dominant factor displayed in the decision tree in Figure 9. If the organization wants to improve service levels they should learn what antecedents determine average speed of answer. For example, this may involve collecting new data, studying how efficient the automatic call distribution system performs.

In Figure 6 below decision-makers can see that average speed of answer accounts for the predictions of over half the terminal nodes. Average speed of answer is also the only variable influencing the first three levels of the decision tree, and most of the fourth level. This demonstrates average speed of answer is very influential in determining service levels. The next most significant variables are abandons and maximum delay; they occupy positions at four decision nodes (two each). Managers should improve call center performance in those areas to provide the most gains in service level. While weekday and average handle time are included in the decision tree they only apply to two decision nodes (non-terminal node) far down in the tree.

The decision tree can provide predictions of future service levels based on current variable values. If current values for variables like average handle time, and average speed of answer stay approximately the same it is reasonable to predict that service levels will not vary much in the future. There are sources of variation in service levels that this decision tree does not account for, but they represent less than 25% of total variation.

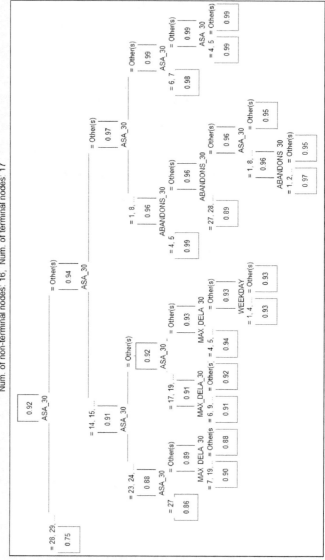

Figure 6: Decision tree with DTIC parameter 0.1
Num. of non-terminal nodes: 16, Num. of terminal nodes: 17

Discussion

The application presented above calculates the information criterion and opportunity loss measures. Results from the analysis demonstrate the range of possibilities resulting from one dataset. Managers use these results to predict future service levels, or isolate the variables with the greatest impact on service level.

We follow the steps for using a mathematical tool in management decision-making (Simon, 1977) and fulfill each of those steps by providing a mathematical model that includes the important factors analyzed. CART and the discretization routine accomplish that step. Next, a decision-maker defines a criterion function in the form of the presented IC. The criterion function and opportunity loss allows for the comparison of different courses of action. A decision-maker collects the empirical estimates of the IC parameter and applies it to the remaining decision trees, maximizing their preference for parsimony and accuracy, enabling better decisions.

The results from this study demonstrate that a decision-maker may rely on the IC to choose a decision tree with the best tradeoff between accuracy and complexity. These results demonstrate that the IC and opportunity loss measures behave as predicted indicating validity of the measures.

Organizations collect data that is appropriate for discretization and decision tree analysis. This application is useful in a variety of business applications including marketing research for segmenting customer groups, loan officers improving credit decisions, and quality control applications. We analyzed service level data from an insurance call center. However, many applications exist in which service levels need to be represented, such as telemarketing, inventories, scheduling job shops or personnel decisions. In these examples the data may result in model subsets. This application provides a good method for managers to improve their decision-making when faced with model   subsets.

Possible extensions of this research include generalizing the IC function to work with a variety of rule induction algorithms, and further exploration of the opportunity loss measure as applied to problems including real estate and abandonment decisions. In addition, one may expand the application to utilize two or more discretization methods, enabling decision-makers to further customize datasets for better personal decisions.

Conclusion

We provide a unique information criterion for evaluating decision trees because it provides an effective and efficient method for model selection. This will enable decision-makers to choose among different decision alternatives (trees) constructed from the same data set. The ability to compare and contrast separate decision trees enables decision-makers to select a model that suits their individual needs. Calculating the opportunity losses among decision trees aids the decision-making process by providing information about the real differences in alternative models. To date there is no competing technique that allows a decision-maker to compare decision trees (model subsets) with different categorization schemes based on the same initial dataset.

Traditionally, information was a scarce factor in decision-making (Simon, 1998). Now, information is plentiful and filtering through it is a challenge. The processes presented in this book are great time saving devices and lead to improved decision-making.

References

Akaike, H. (1976). Canonical correlation analysis of time series and the use of an information criterion. In R. K. Mehra & D. G. Lainiotis (Eds.), *System identification* (pp. 27-96). New York: Academic Press.

Atlason, J., Epelman, M. A., & Henderson, S. G. (2004). Call center staffing with simulation and cutting plan methods. *Annals of Operations Research, 127,* 333-358.

Berka, P., & Bruha, I. (1995). Various discretizing procedures of numerical attributes: Empirical comparisons. In *Proceedings of the 8th European Conference on Workshop Statistics, Machine Learning, and Knowledge Discovery in Databases* (pp. 136-141). Heraklion, Crete.

Besson, J., Robardet, C., Boulicaut, J.-F., & Rome, S. (2005). Constraint-based concept mining and its applicatin to micro array data analysis. *Intelligent Data Analysis, 9*(1), 59-82.

Bozdogan, H. (1987). Model selection and Akaike's information criterion (AIC): The general theory and its analytical extensions. *Psychometrika, 52*(3), 345-370.

Bryson, N., & Joseph, A. (2001). Optimal techniques for class-dependent attribute discretization. *Journal of the Operational Research Society, 52*(10), 1130-1143.

Cherkauer, K. J., & Shavlik, J. W. (1996). Growing simpler decision trees to facilitate knowledge discovery. In *In proceedings of the second international conference on knowledge discovery and data mining.* Portland, OR.

Cyert, R. M., Simon, H. A., & Trow, D. B. (1956). Observation of a business decision. *The Journal of Business, 29*(4), 237-248.

Dougherty, J., Kohavi, R., & Sahami, M. (1995). Supervised and unsupervised discretization of continuous features. In *Proceedings of the Twelfth International Conference on Machine Learning* (pp. 194-202). San Francisco, CA.

Ishibuchi, H., & Yamamoto, T. (2003). Deriving fuzzy discretization from interval discretization. In *Proceedings of the 12th IEEE International Conference on Fuzzy Systems.* St. Louis, MO.

3

Jarrett, J., & Kraft, A. (1989). *Statistical analysis for decision making*. Boston, MA: Allyn and Bacon.

Kros, J. F. (2008). *Spreadsheet modeling for business deicisons*: McGraw-Hill Irwin.

Kurgan, L. A., & Cios, K. J. (2004). CAIM discretization algorithm. *IEEE Transactions on Knowledge and Data Engineering, 16*(2), 145-154.

Kwedlo, W., & Kretowski, M. (1999). An evolutionary algorithm using multivariate discretization for decision rule induction. In *Proceedings of the 8th Workshop on Intelligent Information Systems* (pp. 392-397). Ustron, Poland.

Kyper, E., Lloyd, S., & Chinn, S. (2004). Data Mining: A Restrospective Analysis. In *Proceedings of the 2004 Information Resources Management Association International Conference*. New Orleans, LA.

Liu, L., Wong, A. K. C., & Wang, Y. (2004). A global optimal algorithm for class-dependent discretization of continuous data. *Intelligent Data Analysis, 8*, 151-170.

McClave, J. T., Benson, P. G., & Sincich, T. (2001). *Statistics for Business and Economics* (8th ed.). Upper Saddle River, NJ: Prentice Hall.

Mitchell, T. (1997). Decision tree learning. In *Machine Learning* (pp. 52-78): McGraw-Hill.

Moody, E. A. (1967). William of Ockham. In P. Edwards (Ed.), *The encyclopedia of philosophy*. New York, NY: Macmillan Publishing Co., Inc.

Petersen, H. C., & Lewis, W. C. (1999). *Managerial Economics* (4th ed.). Upper Saddle River, NJ: Prentice-Hall.

Postema, M., Wu, X., & Menzies, T. (1997). A tuning aid for discretization in rule induction. In *Proceedings of the 1997 Pacific-Asia Conference on Knowledge Discovery and Data Mining* (pp. 79-87). Singapore.

Shannon, C. E. (1948). A mathematical theory of communication. *The Bell System Technical Journal, 27*, 379-423.

Simon, H. A. (1977). *The new science of management decision*. Englewood Cliffs, NJ: Prentice-Hall Inc.

Simon, H. A. (1987). Making management decisions: the role of intuition and emotion. *The Academy of Management Executive, 1*(1), 57-64.

Simon, H. A. (1998). Information 101: It's not what you know, it's how you know it. *The Journal for Quality and Participation, 21*(4), 30-33.

Ventura, D., & Martinez, T. R. (1995). An empirical comparison of discretization methods. In *Proceedings of the Tenth International Symposium on Computer and Information Sciences* (pp. 443-450). Izmir, Turkey.

Wei, W. W. S. (1993). *Time series analysis: Univariate and multivariate methods*. Redwood City, CA: Addison-Wesley Publishing Company, Inc.

Winston, P. (1992). Learning by building information trees. In P. Winston (Ed.), *Artificial Intelligence* (pp. 423-442): Addison-Wesley.

Appendix A

Display open file dialogue to user;
Get file name for statistica input file;
If filename is valid statistica datasheet
    Open Statistica data file;
    Prepare data for analysis{
            Display user dialogue for variable selection from statistica data file {
            Select continuous variables;
            Select categorical variables;
            Select dependent variable;

        Display user dialogue for discretization parameters
            Select minimum number of discretization categories;
            Select maximum number of discretization categories;
            Select discretization category increment value;

        For each variable to be discretized
            Sort variable;
            For each category
                Determine category cutpoints;
                Add new discretized variable to statistica data file;

Appendix B
Input for Tables 1 thru 3

R^2	N	DTIC
0.05	5	4.5932
0.10	5	4.4041
0.15	5	4.2150
0.20	5	4.0259
0.25	5	3.8368
0.30	5	3.6476
0.35	5	3.4585
0.40	5	3.2694
0.45	5	3.0803
0.50	5	2.8912
0.55	5	2.7021
0.60	5	2.5129
0.65	5	2.3238
0.70	5	2.1347
0.75	5	1.9456
0.80	5	1.7565
0.85	5	1.5674
0.90	5	1.3782
0.95	5	1.1891
1.00	5	1.0000

Table 1: Inputs and DTIC values for Figure 1

R^2	N	DTIC
0.25	3	4.8464
0.25	4	4.0000
0.25	5	3.8368
0.25	6	3.8392
0.25	7	3.9048
0.25	8	4.0000
0.25	9	4.1107
0.25	10	4.2301
0.25	11	4.3544
0.25	12	4.4817
0.25	13	4.6105
0.25	14	4.7402
0.25	15	4.8701
0.25	16	5.0000
0.25	17	5.1296
0.25	18	5.2588
0.25	19	5.3874
0.25	20	5.5154
0.25	21	5.6428
0.25	22	5.7696

Table 2: Inputs and DTIC values for Figure 2

R^2	N	DTIC
0.05	3	5.8721
0.06	4	4.7600
0.07	5	4.5176
0.08	6	4.4827
0.09	7	4.5245
0.10	8	4.6000
0.11	9	4.6914
0.12	10	4.7900
0.13	11	4.8911
0.14	12	4.9923
0.15	13	5.0919
0.16	14	5.1890
0.17	15	5.2829
0.18	16	5.3733
0.19	17	5.4600
0.20	18	5.5427
0.21	19	5.6214
0.22	20	5.6961
0.23	21	5.7667
0.24	22	5.8332

Table 3: Inputs and DTIC values for Figure 3

Appendix C: Pseudo-code for application

```
Display open file dialogue to user;
Get file name for Statistica input file;
If filename is valid Statistica datasheet {
    Open Statistica data file;
    Prepare data for analysis {
        Display user dialogue for variable selection from Statistica data file {
            Select continuous variables;
            Select categorical variables;
            Select dependent variable;
        }
        Display user dialogue for discretization parameters {
            Select minimum number of discretization categories;
            Select maximum number of discretization categories;
            Select discretization category increment value;
        }
        For each variable to be discretized {
            Sort variable;
            For each category {
                Determine category cutpoints;
                Add new discretized variable to Statistica data file;
            }
        }
    }
    Setup and run CART {
        For each discretized category {
            Pass discretized, categorical, and dependent variables to CART;
            Setup CART parameters and run CART;
        }
    }
    Display results {
        For each CART analysis result {
            Determine number of non-terminal nodes;
            Calculate R squared;
            Calculate IC value with default IC parameter value of 1.0;
        }
        Remove trees with duplicate non-terminal nodes and lowest R squares from CART result set;
        Flag CART result with lowest IC value;
        Display table of IC values, R squared, and tree size;
        Display graph of IC values vs. non-terminal nodes;
        Display user dialogue with optional IC parameter values;
        For each new IC parameter value selected {
            Recalculate IC values for each CART result;
            Flag lowest IC value;
            Display new table with IC values, R squared, and tree size;
        }
    }
}
```

Wissenschaftlicher Buchverlag bietet

kostenfreie

Publikation

von

wissenschaftlichen Arbeiten

Diplomarbeiten, Magisterarbeiten, Master und Bachelor Theses
sowie Dissertationen, Habilitationen und wissenschaftliche Monographien

Sie verfügen über eine wissenschaftliche Abschlußarbeit zu aktuellen oder zeitlosen
Fragestellungen, die hohen inhaltlichen und formalen Ansprüchen genügt,
und haben **Interesse an einer honorarvergüteten Publikation**?

Dann senden Sie bitte erste Informationen über Ihre Arbeit per Email
an info@vdm-verlag.de. Unser Außenlektorat meldet sich umgehend bei Ihnen.

VDM Verlag Dr. Müller Aktiengesellschaft & Co. KG
Dudweiler Landstraße 125a
D - 66123 Saarbrücken

www.vdm-verlag.de

www.ingramcontent.com/pod-product-compliance
Lightning Source LLC
LaVergne TN
LVHW052316060326
832902LV00021B/3920